BASEBALL'S GREATEST PLAYERS

Baseball's

GREATEST PLAYERS

10 BASEBALL BIOGRAPHIES FOR NEW READERS

· · · · · · · · · · · · · · · · · ·

Andrew Martin

· · · · · · · · · · · · · · · · · ·

Illustrations by Claudio Cerri

CALLISTO
PUBLISHING

**FOR JOSHELYN,
WITH WHOM ALL THINGS
ARE POSSIBLE.**

CONTENTS

INTRODUCTION

I first came to love baseball as a kid. I started collecting baseball cards that came in boxes of cereal. From there, going to games and watching them on television helped me fall in love with how exciting the sport is. There is nothing better than baseball!

Baseball's Greatest Players highlights the players that I believe are the best from each decade during the past 100 years. There is no official list of the best players. My choices are based on my opinion of who has the most impressive stats and those who made the greatest impact on the game, those who played with them, and those who watched them.

You don't have to be a baseball fan to read and enjoy *Baseball's Greatest Players*. Because each player impacted those who came after, reading in

order helps tell the
story best. There
is also a glossary in
the back of the book
(page 61) that explains
some baseball terms
and other words you
may not be familiar with.

If I have done my job
right, you will have a
better understanding
and love of baseball
after reading *Baseball's
Greatest Players*. Most
important, you will
have questions you
want to continue
exploring about these
players and others who have
helped make baseball an American treasure.
In that case, consider exploring the Resources
section (page 64).

Babe Ruth

1895-1948

BABE RUTH

1895-1948

Babe Ruth was baseball's most legendary player. Babe hit so many home runs that he changed **Major League Baseball** forever and became famous around the world.

George Herman Ruth was born in Baltimore, Maryland. As George got older, people called him Babe because he looked and acted like a big kid. The name stuck. When he was young, he often got into trouble. His parents sent him to live at a reform

SUPER STATS

POSITION:
OUTFIELDER/PITCHER

TEAMS:
BOSTON RED SOX: 1914-1919
NEW YORK YANKEES: 1920-1934
BOSTON BRAVES: 1935

BATTING AVERAGE:
.342

HITS:
2,873

HOME RUNS:
714

RUNS BATTED IN (RBIs):
2,214

PITCHING WINS:
94

school called St. Mary's. It was there that one of his teachers, Brother Mathias, changed his life.

Brother Mathias taught Babe how to play baseball and to hit. Babe learned to throw and hit left-handed. He was a great hitter but also a talented pitcher.

In 1914, when he was just 19, Babe made the major leagues as a pitcher with the Boston Red Sox. Babe was soon one of the team's best pitchers.

Because he hit so well, Babe sometimes played outfield. At that time, players didn't hit a lot of home runs, but Babe changed that.

In 1918, Babe played outfield more than he pitched. He led the league in home runs, and in 1919, he hit almost 30 home runs, more than any major league player had hit so far!

The New York Yankees bought Babe's **contract** from the Red Sox after the 1919 season. They believed Babe would help them win games and be popular with fans. They were right! Babe played outfield for the Yankees. Soon, he was the best player in baseball. He became very popular because of his home runs.

When Yankee Stadium first opened in 1923, people called it the "House that Ruth Built" because of how important Babe was to the team. Babe's baseball talent was the main reason why his teams won a lot of games and championships. He won three **World Series** with the Red Sox and then won four more with New York.

After 22 years, Babe retired from playing in 1935. Babe had a .342 lifetime **batting average** with 714 home runs, 2,873 hits and 2,214 **runs batted in (RBIs)**. For many years, he had the most home runs and RBIs of any player. He also won 94 games as a pitcher, with a 2.28 **earned run average (ERA)** and 488 strikeouts.

Babe was one of the first players voted into the **Baseball Hall of Fame** and was baseball's first big home run hitter.

Babe made baseball more exciting and changed it forever! That's why he is still one of the game's biggest stars.

RUNNERS UP

ROGERS HORNSBY: The second baseman played mostly for the St. Louis Cardinals. Rogers batted .358 during his career and led the league in batting average seven times.

DAZZY VANCE: Dazzy was a star right-handed pitcher with the Brooklyn Dodgers. He won 197 games with a 3.24 ERA, leading the league in strikeouts seven times.

Lou Gehrig

1903-1941

LOU GEHRIG

....
1903-1941
....

Playing baseball can be hard. But as star first baseman for the New York Yankees, Lou Gehrig made it look easy, almost never missing a game.

Lou was born and grew up in New York City after his parents came from Germany. He didn't learn to speak English until he was five. Lou helped his family earn money by doing odd jobs as a kid, but he still found time to play sports. Lou was very good at

SUPER STATS

POSITION:
FIRST BASE

TEAM:
NEW YORK YANKEES: 1923-1939

BATTING AVERAGE:
.340

HITS:
2,721

HOME RUNS:
493

RUNS BATTED IN (RBIs):
1,995

RUNS SCORED:
1,888

football but even better at baseball. Playing first base and pitching, he batted and threw left-handed.

Lou also did well in school, attending college at Columbia University in New York. He played for the school's baseball team, where he started getting a lot of attention for how well he played.

In 1923, the New York Yankees were the most popular sports team in the world. They already had outfielder Babe Ruth and wanted another star player to join him, so they decided to sign Lou to a contract.

Lou was young, so he spent most of 1923 and 1924 in the **minor leagues** to get experience. By 1925, he had played so well that he was the Yankees' first baseman, and it wasn't long before he was as big of a star as Babe.

Usually hitting **cleanup**, Lou led the **American League** in batting average once, in home runs three times, and in RBIs five times. He also won the **Most Valuable Player (MVP) Award** in 1927 and 1936. While Lou was on the team, the Yankees played in seven different World Series, winning six.

Lou played in an amazing 2,130 straight games. Players usually got hurt or needed rest, but not Lou. He held the record for most consecutive games played until Baltimore Orioles' shortstop Cal Ripken broke that record in 1995. The ability to play every day helped Lou get the nickname "The Iron Horse."

In 1938, Lou started to feel tired and sick, and by the next season, he could barely swing his bat. Doctors found that Lou had a disease in his nerves and brain that meant he had to stop playing.

During Lou's 17 years with the Yankees, he had a .340 batting average, 493 home runs, and 1,995 RBIs. He was selected to the Baseball Hall of Fame in 1939.

When Lou played his last game at Yankee Stadium, he told fans he was the luckiest man on the face of the earth despite his sickness, which became known as Lou Gehrig's disease and is now called ALS. Lou died in 1941 when he was only 37.

Lou was one of the best players ever because of his hitting, leadership, and ability to play in so many games. For all of these reasons and more, he was loved by many.

RUNNERS UP

JIMMIE FOXX: A right-handed first baseman for the Philadelphia Athletics and Boston Red Sox. Jimmie hit .325 with 534 home runs and won three MVP Awards.

LEFTY GROVE: The left-handed pitcher won 300 games with a 3.06 ERA for the Philadelphia Athletics and Boston Red Sox. He led the league in strikeouts seven times.

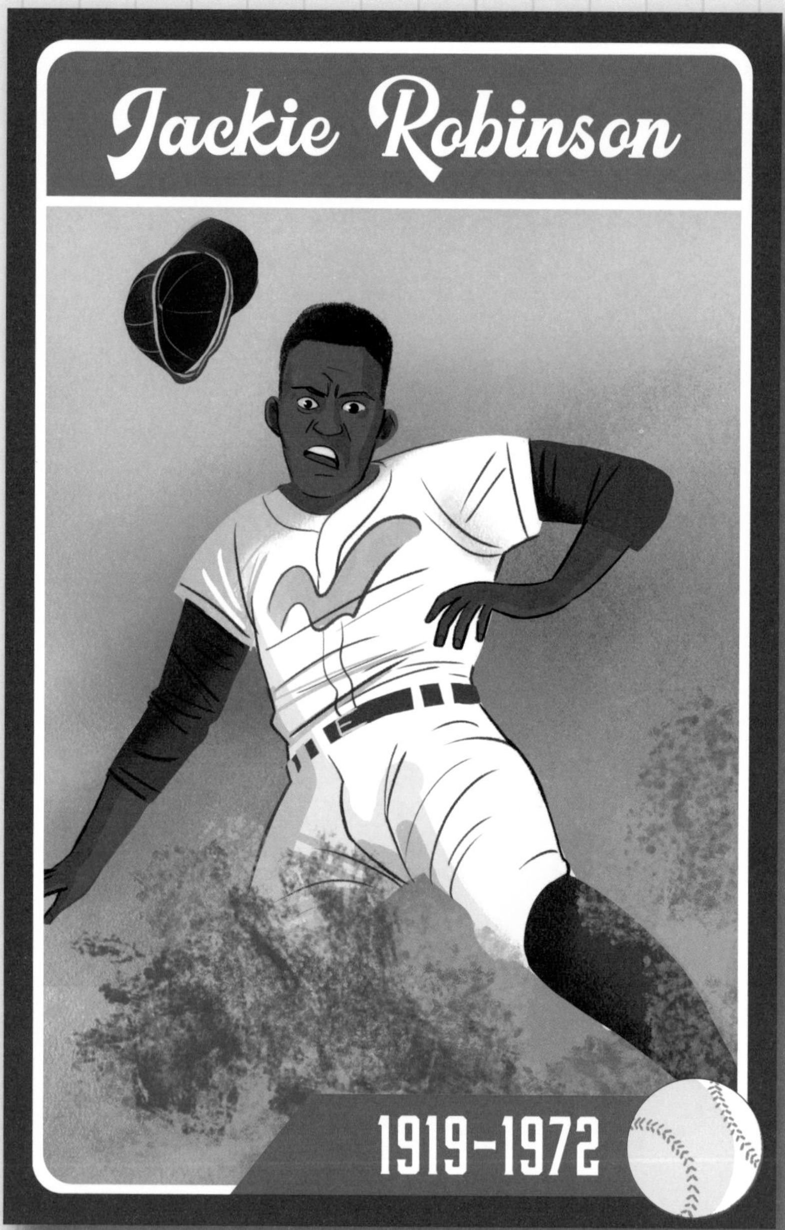
Jackie Robinson
1919–1972

JACKIE ROBINSON

1919–1972

Few baseball players ever faced more challenges than Jackie Robinson. But he wouldn't give up. He became one of the game's biggest stars because he was so brave and determined.

Jackie's parents were poor farmers from Georgia, where the family experienced **racism** because they were Black. When he was young, the family moved to California. He and his four brothers and sisters all played sports, and his brother Mack won a silver medal as a runner at the 1936 Olympics.

SUPER STATS

POSITION:
SECOND BASE

TEAMS:
KANSAS CITY MONARCHS: 1945–1946
BROOKLYN DODGERS: 1947–1956

BATTING AVERAGE:
.311

HITS:
1,518

HOME RUNS:
137

RUNS BATTED IN (RBIs):
734

RUNS SCORED:
946

In addition to playing baseball, football, and basketball and running track, Jackie was a great student. He attended college at UCLA and then was in the army for two years.

After leaving the army, Jackie began playing professional football but decided a baseball career was what he really wanted. Major League Baseball didn't allow Black players at that time, so Jackie played in the **Negro Leagues**, for the Kansas City Monarchs, instead. He was right-handed and had a .375 batting average in 1945, which got him a lot of attention.

Branch Rickey, the general manager of the Brooklyn Dodgers, thought it was wrong to keep Black players out of Major League Baseball. He decided to sign Jackie because he knew how talented and tough he was. Branch believed Jackie would play well even when things were difficult.

Jackie joined the Dodgers in 1947. It was very hard from the beginning because he was called names and treated badly. He often couldn't eat at restaurants or stay at hotels with his teammates because he was Black, but he didn't fight back and started making people quiet by showing them how well he played.

As a **rookie** with the Dodgers, Jackie played first base, hitting .297 and leading the **National League** with 29 **stolen bases**. The Dodgers made the World Series that year but lost to the New York Yankees. At the end of the season, Jackie won the first-ever **Rookie of the Year Award**.

In 10 seasons with the Dodgers, Jackie made six **All-Star** teams and his team finished first or second every year but one. He played in six different World Series, winning one. When the Dodgers moved to Los Angeles in 1957, Jackie retired instead of going with them.

Jackie was a great player and his bravery as the first Black player in Major League Baseball made him a role model for many fans and players. He was very deserving of being voted into the Hall of Fame in 1962.

Major League Baseball retired Jackie's uniform number 42, so it can never be worn again by another player. April 15 was also named Jackie Robinson Day. Each year on that day, all major league teams celebrate Jackie and what he meant to the game.

JOE DIMAGGIO: A popular outfielder with the New York Yankees, he hit .325 with 361 home runs and won nine World Series.

TED WILLIAMS: Known for a beautiful left-handed swing, the Boston Red Sox's outfielder hit .344 with 521 home runs and won six batting titles in 19 seasons.

Willie Mays

1931–

1950s

WILLIE
MAYS

·········
1931–
·········

E ven the best baseball players usually have a weakness. But one player who seemed to do it all was Willie Mays, one of the game's biggest stars.

Growing up in Alabama, Willie was a great athlete. His father, Cat, was a talented baseball player but never got a chance to play Major League Baseball because he was Black and Jackie Robinson had not yet broken **baseball's color line** in the major leagues.

SUPER STATS

POSITION:
CENTER FIELD

TEAMS:
BIRMINGHAM BLACK BARONS: 1948–1950
NEW YORK GIANTS: 1951–1952; 1954–1957
SAN FRANCISCO GIANTS: 1958–1972
NEW YORK METS: 1972–1973

BATTING AVERAGE:
.302

HITS:
3,283

HOME RUNS:
660

RUNS BATTED IN (RBIs):
1,903

RUNS SCORED:
2,062

Baseball wasn't the only sport Willie played. He was also very good at basketball and football and starred in all three sports for his high school teams.

Beginning in 1948, when he was still in high school, Willie was so good that he played baseball in the Negro Leagues, for the Birmingham Black Barons. But in 1950, after he graduated from school, he signed with the New York Giants.

Willie was immediately a star, winning the 1951 National League Rookie of the Year Award. He was fast, could hit for power, and made difficult plays in the field look easy.

Although Willie spent most of the next two years in the army, he was even better when he returned in 1954. That year, he led the league in hitting and won the MVP Award. The Giants also won the World Series.

During that World Series, Willie made one of the most famous plays in baseball history. Vic Wertz of the Cleveland Indians hit a ball far over Willie's head in center field. Willie ran as fast as he could and caught the ball over his shoulder at the last moment. He quickly threw the ball back to stop runners from scoring, which helped the Giants win the game.

Willie won another MVP Award in 1965 and was an All-Star 20 times. He also won 12 **Gold Glove Awards** for his excellent defense.

Because he was shy and didn't say much as a younger player, Willie was given the nickname "The Say Hey Kid." He didn't need to talk much because his talent made him a favorite of many fans and players.

Willie's 660 home runs are still the sixth most by any major league player ever and he is 12th in both hits and RBIs.

Willie was voted into the Baseball Hall of Fame in 1979 and a large statue of him stands outside of the Giants' Oracle Park in San Francisco. In 1998, the *Sporting News* named him the second greatest player ever, behind only Babe Ruth. It's safe to say Willie will never be forgotten.

RUNNERS UP

MICKEY MANTLE: The **switch-hitting** outfielder won three MVP Awards and seven World Series while hitting 536 home runs for the New York Yankees.

WARREN SPAHN: The left-handed pitcher from the Boston/Milwaukee Braves won 20 or more games in a season 13 times. He finished his career with 363 wins and a 3.09 ERA.

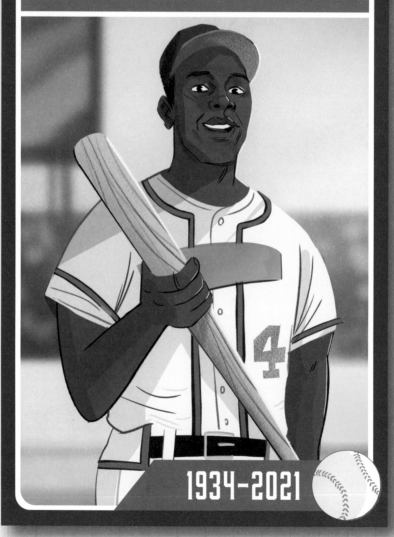

Hank Aaron

1934-2021

HANK AARON

1934-2021

Hank Aaron broke many records during his amazing baseball career. However, he became a hero because of how he played and how he stood up to racism during his life.

Hank grew up loving baseball, but his family was poor. Unable to buy balls and bats, he often played using sticks and bottle caps instead.

Jackie Robinson was Hank's favorite baseball player when he was a kid. He was also Black and

SUPER STATS

POSITION:
RIGHT FIELD

TEAMS:
INDIANAPOLIS CLOWNS: 1952
BOSTON BRAVES: 1952-1954
MILWAUKEE BRAVES: 1954-1965
ATLANTA BRAVES: 1966-1974
MILWAUKEE BREWERS: 1975-1976

BATTING AVERAGE:
.305

HITS:
3,771

HOME RUNS:
755

RUNS BATTED IN (RBIs):
2,297

RUNS SCORED:
2,174

right-handed and was a strong example to him and many others fighting against unfairness and racism.

When Hank was younger, he was a good player but he held his bat wrong, placing his left hand above his right hand. After he changed that, he got even better. Because his high school didn't have a baseball team, he played for an all-Black team in the Negro Leagues, the Indianapolis Clowns, instead.

In 1952, when Hank was just 18, he signed with the Boston Braves (eventually becoming the Milwaukee Braves and then the Atlanta Braves). He spent two years playing in the minor leagues and did well even though he constantly faced racism. Hank remained strong and joined the Milwaukee Braves in 1954, playing most of his games in right field.

Hank was a great hitter who was fast and hit lots of home runs. It was difficult to throw pitches past him because he swung his bat so fast. He hit the ball so hard that he earned the nickname "The Hammer."

It wasn't long before Hank was one of baseball's biggest stars. He made 21 All-Star teams and led the league in batting average twice and in home runs three times. Hank also won the National League MVP Award in 1957, which was the same year the Braves won the World Series.

As Hank neared the end of his baseball career, he was close to Babe Ruth's famous record for the most home runs in baseball history of 714. Many people cheered for Hank to break Babe's record, but others booed him and sent him racist notes and threats because they didn't want a Black man to have the record.

Playing with all the stress, Hank broke the home run record in 1974. He finished his career with 755 home runs, which was a record until 2007 when it was broken by outfielder Barry Bonds of the San Francisco Giants.

After 23 seasons, Hank retired from playing. He had a .305 batting average and 2,297 RBIs, which is still the most ever by one player.

Hank was voted into the Baseball Hall of Fame in 1982. Throughout the rest of his life, Hank continued working in baseball and fighting against racism and the unfair treatment of others. Hank was a true hero in baseball and in life.

RUNNERS UP

BOB GIBSON: The hard-throwing right-handed pitcher won 251 games with a 2.91 ERA in 17 seasons for the St. Louis Cardinals. He was also twice named World Series MVP.

SANDY KOUFAX: In 12 seasons with the Brooklyn/Los Angeles Dodgers, the left-handed pitcher had an ERA of 2.76 and won three **Cy Young Awards**. He was feared for his fastball and curve ball.

ROBERTO CLEMENTE

1934-1972

Roberto Clemente was one of the best players to ever play Major League Baseball. His talent as an outfielder and his kindness made him famous around the world.

Roberto was born in Puerto Rico as one of seven children. The Clemente family was poor. Sometimes, Roberto and his brothers helped their father load trucks with sugarcane for extra money, which they used to buy baseball equipment.

SUPER STATS

POSITION:
RIGHT FIELD

TEAMS:
BROOKLYN DODGERS: 1954
PITTSBURGH PIRATES: 1955-1972

BATTING AVERAGE:
.317

HITS:
3,000

HOME RUNS:
240

RUNS BATTED IN (RBIs):
1,305

RUNS SCORED:
1,416

In school, Roberto played baseball and ran track and field. He ran and threw javelin, but being able to run fast and throw far made him a better baseball player. He was so good that he started playing professionally in Puerto Rico in 1952 when he was only 18.

The Brooklyn Dodgers were the first big-league team to sign Roberto. They thought he was talented but sent him to Canada to play in the minor leagues because he was so young and needed more experience.

The food and weather were very different from what Roberto was used to, and he only spoke Spanish. It was hard not being able to talk with others who only spoke English or French. Roberto didn't play well that first year and the Dodgers weren't sure he would ever be ready to play for their team.

The Pittsburgh Pirates believed Roberto would be a star and he joined their team in 1955 to play right field. As he learned to speak English, he became more comfortable, which helped him play better and show how talented he really was.

Roberto was a right-handed batter who hit for high average. He was also an outstanding fielder who could throw the ball as far as anyone. It wasn't long before he was Pittsburgh's best player.

Playing for Pittsburgh for his entire career, Roberto was so good that he played in 15 All-Star Games and won the 1966 MVP Award. He also had the best batting average in the National League four times and won 12 Gold Glove Awards for his defense. The Pirates won two World Series, with Roberto batting .362.

On New Year's Eve 1972, Roberto heard about a hurricane in Nicaragua. He was known for always helping people, so it wasn't a surprise when he bought supplies and got on a plane to deliver them to people in need. Sadly, Roberto's plane crashed into the ocean and he died.

Roberto is considered by many to be Puerto Rico's best baseball player ever and was voted into the Baseball Hall of Fame in 1973.

RUNNERS UP

JOHNNY BENCH: The powerful right-handed catcher played 17 seasons with the Cincinnati Reds. A two-time MVP, Johnny hit 389 home runs and was a great defensive player.

TOM SEAVER: The right-handed pitcher had 311 wins with a 2.86 ERA in 20 seasons, primarily with the New York Mets and Cincinnati Reds. He also won three Cy Young Awards and is sixth all-time in strikeouts.

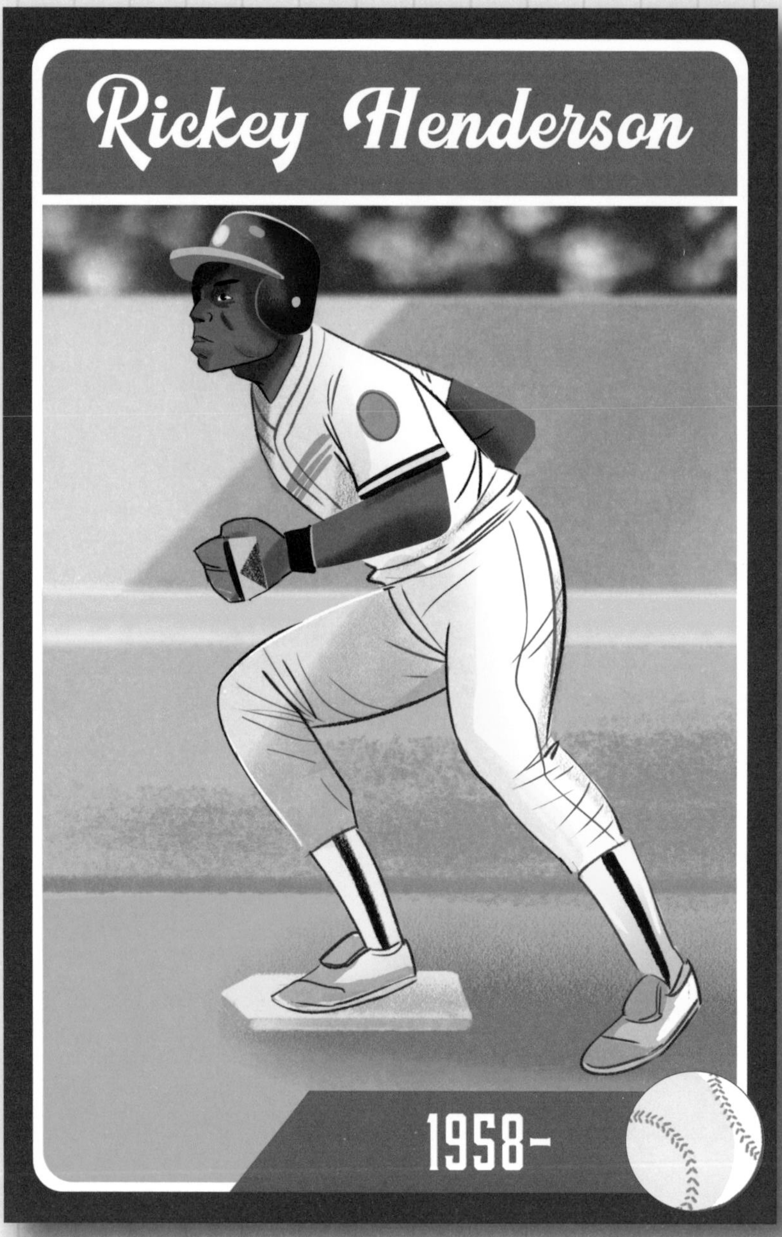
Rickey Henderson
1958-

RICKEY HENDERSON

1958–

It's important for a baseball team to have a good first batter. No **leadoff hitter** has done it any better or for longer than Rickey Henderson.

Rickey's family moved to Oakland, California, when he was young. He starred in sports in school, playing basketball, football, and baseball.

Although Rickey threw left-handed, he taught himself to bat right-handed as a kid so he could be like most of his friends. Soon he was able to hit better than all of them.

SUPER STATS

POSITION:
LEFT FIELD

TEAMS:
OAKLAND A'S: 1976–1984; 1989–1995; 1998
NEW YORK YANKEES: 1985–1989
TORONTO BLUE JAYS: 1993
SAN DIEGO PADRES: 1996–1997; 2001
ANAHEIM ANGELS: 1997
NEW YORK METS: 1999–2000
SEATTLE MARINERS: 2000
BOSTON RED SOX: 2002
LOS ANGELES DODGERS: 2003

BATTING AVERAGE:
.279

HITS:
3,055

HOME RUNS:
297

RUNS BATTED IN (RBIs):
1,115

RUNS SCORED:
2,295

Rickey was great at football but he thought he had a better chance to play baseball professionally. The Oakland A's agreed. They thought he was a special player because of how he could hit and run, so they picked him in the 1976 baseball **draft** when he was only 18.

When Rickey reached the major leagues with Oakland in 1979, after a few years in the minor leagues, he was quickly a star. He seemed to always be on base and running. When he batted, he crouched down low and gave himself a smaller **strike zone** than most hitters.

Rickey usually batted first for his team because he was so good at getting on base and scoring runs. He led off games with a home run 81 times during his career, which is a baseball record!

Speed was where Rickey was truly special. Nobody stole more bases. He stole 100 bases in 1980 and then 130 in 1982, which was the most in one season since 1887.

Rickey led the league in stolen bases 12 times during his career. People called him "The Man of Steal," and in 1991, he broke Lou Brock's record of 938 stolen bases.

Rickey was an All-Star 10 times and won the American League MVP Award in 1990 with Oakland.

During an incredible 25 seasons in the major leagues, Rickey had 1,406 stolen bases, which is still the most ever. He also has the most runs scored with 2,295 and is second in walks with 2,190. He was a part of two World Series championships and was selected to the Baseball Hall of Fame in 2009. A large statue outside of the A's Oakland Coliseum is a reminder to everyone about his greatness.

Since he stopped playing, he has stayed active in baseball as a coach. He remains the all-time stolen base leader and greatest leadoff hitter the game has ever seen.

WADE BOGGS: The left-handed hitting third baseman led the league in batting average five times. Wade batted .328 for his career and made the Hall of Fame in 2005. His 18-year career was primarily spent with the Boston Red Sox and New York Yankees.

DALE MURPHY: A very popular outfielder, mostly with the Atlanta Braves, Dale was a right-handed hitter who won two MVP Awards and hit 398 home runs in his 18-year career.

Frank Thomas

1968-

FRANK THOMAS

....
1968–
....

Many baseball players are big and strong. Frank Thomas is so big and strong that he was called "The Big Hurt," and he became one of the game's best power hitters.

Frank grew up in Georgia. In high school, he was a tight end in football and played first base in baseball. He became well known for being a good athlete.

Frank went to Auburn University to play football. He only played a few games his first year before he got

SUPER STATS

POSITION:
FIRST BASE AND DESIGNATED HITTER

TEAMS:
CHICAGO WHITE SOX: 1989-2005
OAKLAND A'S: 2006-2007
TORONTO BLUE JAYS: 2007-2008

BATTING AVERAGE:
.301

HITS:
2,468

HOME RUNS:
521

RUNS BATTED IN (RBIs):
1,704

RUNS SCORED:
1,494

hurt and decided he would only play baseball from that point on.

After three years starring for Auburn's baseball team, Frank was picked by the Chicago White Sox in the first round of the 1989 baseball draft.

Frank was a special player, especially because of his size. A right-handed batter, he was 6'5" and 250 pounds. At the plate, Frank was patient, hitting for a high batting average with lots of home runs. After only two years in the minor leagues, he joined Chicago and started his major league career.

Frank never stopped hitting once he joined Chicago. He batted .330 as a rookie in 1990 and had a batting average above .300 in 10 of his first 11 seasons.

Because he was so big, Frank wasn't the best at fielding. He sometimes played first base but was also often used as a **designated hitter**.

Frank won the American League MVP Award in 1993 and 1994, and then won the 1995 home run derby at that year's All-Star Game.

After missing most of the 2001 season because of a bad muscle injury, Frank returned and hit 28 home runs the next season. It was a reminder to other players that he was still "The Big Hurt."

Late in his career, Frank left Chicago and played for a couple of other teams. He did well but wasn't playing as well and kept getting hurt. He finally retired after the 2008 season.

Frank had eight seasons with at least 35 home runs, 10 seasons with at least 100 RBIs, and he led the league in walks four times.

Frank is one of only nine players to finish with a batting average above .300 and have more than 500 home runs, which helped him get voted into the Hall of Fame in 2014. There is now a statue of him outside of the White Sox stadium.

Since Frank stopped playing, he has stayed in baseball, working as an announcer during games and also appearing in commercials.

RUNNERS UP

KEN GRIFFEY, JR.: The left-handed hitting center fielder was a 13-time All-Star and led the league in home runs four times during his 22-year career. The majority of his career was spent with the Seattle Mariners and Cincinnati Reds. His father was former big-league player Ken Griffey, Sr.

TONY GWYNN: A right fielder, the left-handed hitter spent his entire 20-year career with the San Diego Padres, hitting .338 and winning eight batting titles.

Derek Jeter

1974-

DEREK JETER

....

1974–

....

Baseball has had some great players who were also amazing leaders. Shortstop Derek Jeter was so good at both while playing with the New York Yankees that he was simply called "The Captain."

Derek grew up in Michigan. When he was young, his parents wanted to make sure he never gave up on anything, so he wasn't allowed to use the word "can't." This helped him learn that anything is possible.

SUPER STATS

POSITION:
SHORTSTOP

TEAM:
NEW YORK YANKEES: 1992–2014

BATTING AVERAGE:
.310

HITS:
3,465

HOME RUNS:
260

RUNS BATTED IN (RBIs):
1,311

RUNS SCORED:
1,923

Derek was a star shortstop in school who batted right-handed. He also ran track and played basketball, but baseball was clearly his best sport. He was so good that the University of Michigan, his hometown school, gave him a scholarship to play for them.

Before Derek went to college, the New York Yankees made him their first pick in the 1992 baseball draft. Because Derek was so young, he spent several years playing in the minor leagues to get ready for the major leagues. Derek finally joined the Yankees in 1995 and showed he was ready to be their starting shortstop.

Derek ended up playing for the Yankees for 20 years and had one of the best careers in baseball history. He won the Rookie of the Year Award in 1996 and was an All-Star 14 times. He was such a good leader that the Yankees made him their **captain** in 2003, only the 15th captain in team history.

New York went to the playoffs 16 times during his career and won five World Series. This helped him get another nickname, "Mr. November." Derek seemed to play even better when there was the most pressure, as he batted .321 in the seven World Series.

In addition to winning a lot, he also became known for making plays that at first looked like they might be impossible, like diving into the stands or making difficult throws.

It was no surprise when Derek joined the Baseball Hall of Fame in 2020. There have been few players as popular and talented as he was. There really wasn't anything he couldn't do, just like his parents taught him.

Since Derek stopped playing, he has stayed in baseball. In 2017, he was part of a group that bought the Miami Marlins of the National League. He is now in charge of the team, and in 2020, the Marlins made the playoffs for the first time since 2003, showing how Derek still won't say "can't."

ALBERT PUJOLS: A power-hitting first baseman who is still playing as of 2021, Albert has more than 3,000 hits, 2,000 RBIs, and is nearing 700 home runs during his over 21-year career. He has played for the St. Louis Cardinals, Los Angeles Angels (2012–2021), and Los Angeles Dodgers (present).

ICHIRO SUZUKI: After 10 seasons playing professionally in Japan, the left-handed outfielder played 19 major league seasons, mostly with the Seattle Mariners, hitting .311 with 3,089 hits and 509 stolen bases.

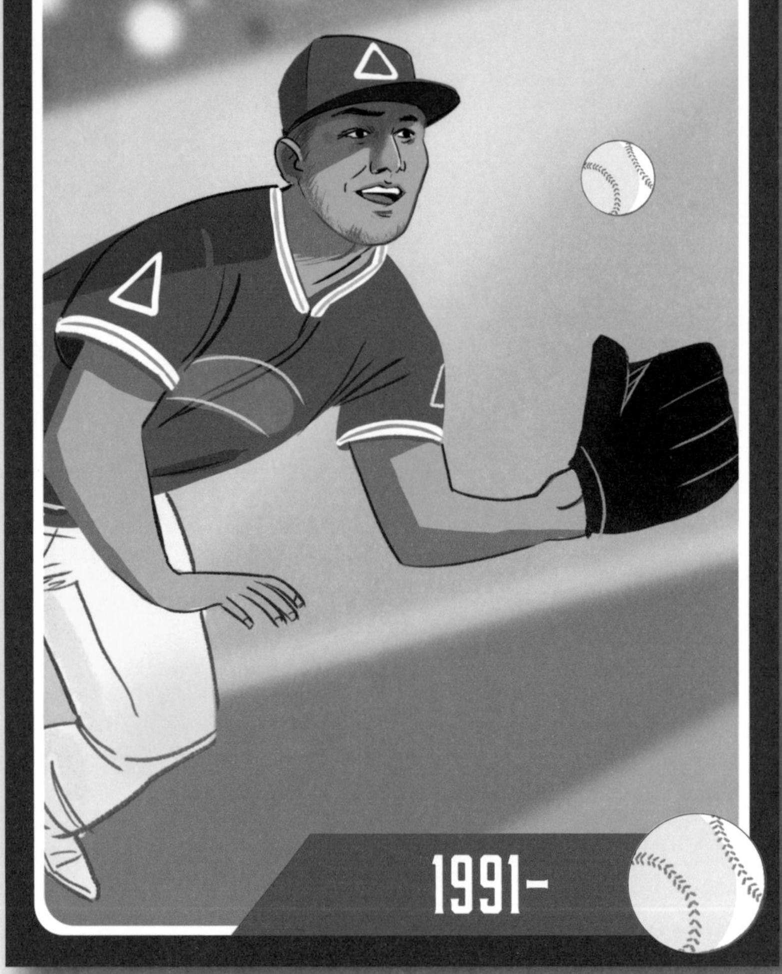
Mike Trout
1991-

MIKE TROUT

········
1991–
········

I t's very hard to be good at more than just one thing in baseball. Mike Trout is a huge star because there isn't much he can't do on the field.

Mike grew up in New Jersey. His father, Jeff, played second base in the minor leagues for four seasons in the 1980s after being drafted by the Minnesota Twins. Although he didn't make the major leagues, he passed his love of the game on to his son.

Originally a shortstop and pitcher, Mike moved to the outfield in high school. A right-handed hitter with

SUPER STATS

POSITION:
CENTER FIELD

TEAM:
LOS ANGELES ANGELS: 2011–

BATTING AVERAGE:
.305

HITS:
1,419

HOME RUNS:
310

RUNS BATTED IN (RBIs):
816

RUNS SCORED:
967

power, Mike was so good he couldn't be ignored, and the Los Angeles Angels drafted him in the first round in 2009.

Even though Mike was still a teenager, he played so well in the minor leagues that the Angels put him on their team in 2011 when he was just 19. The Angels made Mike their starting center fielder in 2012, and he responded by winning the Rookie of the Year Award and finishing second in MVP voting!

Mike quickly showed he was a **five-tool player** and one of the best players in the game. Since joining the Angels, Mike has hit more than 30 home runs in a season six different times and batted over .300 five times, which has helped him win three MVP Awards, finish second four times, and make nine All-Star teams.

Unfortunately, the Angels have only made the playoffs once during his career, and that was a three-game series they lost in 2014.

With Mike signed to a huge 12-year, $426.5 million contract, which is more money than any baseball player has ever been paid, he could be with Los Angeles for the rest of his career.

Mike already holds many Angels' team records, including most home runs. Because he has not won a championship, winning a World Series will be a major goal for him and the Angels.

Because of how much he has already done, Mike is well on his way to being one of the best players in the history of baseball. He is already pretty certain of one day being voted into the Hall of Fame, but what he does during his final seasons will really set his legacy.

RUNNERS UP

MOOKIE BETTS: Another five-tool player, the right-handed outfielder has won an MVP Award and two World Series while with the Boston Red Sox and the Los Angeles Dodgers. He joined the Los Angeles Dodgers in 2020, signing a $365 million contract.

BUSTER POSEY: The catcher has been the face of the San Francisco Giants since 2009. A right-handed hitter, he has won a batting title, an MVP Award, and three World Series.